CAPE EDITIONS 48

Chamber Music

James Joyce

JONATHAN CAPE
THIRTY BEDFORD SQUARE
LONDON

Available in the United States from Grossman Publishers, Inc.

First published 1907
First published in this format 1971, reset from the edition published by Jonathan Cape in 1927
Jonathan Cape Ltd, 30 Bedford Square, London WC1

CAPE Paperback edition ISBN 0 224 00605 3
Hardback edition ISBN 0 224 00606 1

GROSSMAN Paperback edition SBN 670 21127 3
Hardback edition SBN 670 21126 5

LCCC 76-170611

Printed and bound in Great Britain
by Richard Clay (The Chaucer Press), Ltd,
Bungay, Suffolk

I

Strings in the earth and air
   Make music sweet;
Strings by the river where
   The willows meet.

There's music along the river
   For Love wanders there,
Pale flowers on his mantle,
   Dark leaves on his hair.

All softly playing,
   With head to the music bent,
And fingers straying
   Upon an instrument.

II

The twilight turns from amethyst
  To deep and deeper blue,
The lamp fills with a pale green glow
  The trees of the avenue.

The old piano plays an air,
  Sedate and slow and gay;
She bends upon the yellow keys,
  Her head inclines this way.

Shy thoughts and grave wide eyes and hands
  That wander as they list –
The twilight turns to darker blue
  With lights of amethyst.

III

At that hour when all things have repose,
   O lonely watcher of the skies,
   Do you hear the night wind and the sighs
Of harps playing unto Love to unclose
   The pale gates of sunrise?

When all things repose do you alone
   Awake to hear the sweet harps play
   To Love before him on his way,
And the night wind answering in antiphon
   Till night is overgone?

Play on, invisible harps, unto Love
   Whose way in heaven is aglow
   At that hour when soft lights come and go,
Soft sweet music in the air above
   And in the earth below.

IV

When the shy star goes forth in heaven
   All maidenly, disconsolate,
Hear you amid the drowsy even
   One who is singing by your gate.
His song is softer than the dew
   And he is come to visit you.

O bend no more in revery
   When he at eventide is calling
Nor muse : Who may this singer be
   Whose song about my heart is falling?
Know you by this, the lover's chant,
   'Tis I that am your visitant.

V

Lean out of the window,
   Goldenhair,
I heard you singing
   A merry air.

My book is closed,
   I read no more,
Watching the fire dance
   On the floor.

I have left my book :
   I have left my room :
For I heard you singing
   Through the gloom,

Singing and singing
   A merry air.
Lean out of the window,
   Goldenhair.

VI

I would in that sweet bosom be
    (O sweet it is and fair it is!)
Where no rude wind might visit me.
    Because of sad austerities
I would in that sweet bosom be.

I would be ever in that heart
    (O soft I knock and soft entreat her!)
Where only peace might be my part.
    Austerities were all the sweeter
So I were ever in that heart.

VII

My love is in a light attire
  Among the appletrees
Where the gay winds do most desire
  To run in companies.

There, where the gay winds stay to woo
  The young leaves as they pass,
My love goes slowly, bending to
  Her shadow on the grass;

And where the sky's a pale blue cup
  Over the laughing land,
My love goes lightly, holding up
  Her dress with dainty hand.

VIII

Who goes amid the green wood
  With springtide all adorning her?
Who goes amid the merry green wood
  To make it merrier?

Who passes in the sunlight
  By ways that know the light footfall?
Who passes in the sweet sunlight
  With mien so virginal?

The ways of all the woodland
  Gleam with a soft and golden fire –
For whom does all the sunny woodland
  Carry so brave attire?

O, it is for my true love
  The woods their rich apparel wear –
O, it is for my own true love,
  That is so young and fair.

IX

Winds of May, that dance on the sea,
  Dancing a ringaround in glee
From furrow to furrow, while overhead
The foam flies up to be garlanded
In silvery arches spanning the air,
Saw you my true love anywhere?
          Welladay! Welladay!
          For the winds of May!
  Love is unhappy when love is away!

X

Bright cap and streamers,
He sings in the hollow :
Come follow, come follow,
All you that love.
Leave dreams to the dreamers
That will not after,
That song and laughter
Do nothing move.

With ribbons streaming
He sings the bolder;
In troop at his shoulder
The wild bees hum.
And the time of dreaming
Dreams is over –
As lover to lover,
Sweetheart, I come.

XI

Bid adieu, adieu, adieu,
  Bid adieu to girlish days.
Happy Love is come to woo
  Thee and woo thy girlish ways –
The zone that doth become thee fair,
The snood upon thy yellow hair,

When thou hast heard his name upon
  The bugles of the cherubim
Begin thou softly to unzone
Thy girlish bosom unto him
And softly to undo the snood
That is the sign of maidenhood.

XII

What counsel has the hooded moon
  Put in thy heart, my shyly sweet,
Of Love in ancient plenilune,
  Glory and stars beneath his feet –
A sage that is but kith and kin
With the comedian capuchin?

Believe me rather that am wise
  In disregard of the divine.
A glory kindles in those eyes,
  Trembles to starlight. Mine, O mine!
No more be tears in moon or mist
For thee, sweet sentimentalist.

XIII

Go seek her out all courteously
  And say I come,
Wind of spices whose song is ever
  Epithalamium.
O, hurry over the dark lands
  And run upon the sea
For seas and lands shall not divide us,
  My love and me.

Now, wind, of your good courtesy
  I pray you go
And come into her little garden
  And sing at her window;
Singing: The bridal wind is blowing
  For Love is at his noon;
And soon will your true love be with you,
  Soon, O soon.

XIV

My dove, my beautiful one,
Arise, arise!
The nightdew lies
Upon my lips and eyes.

The odorous winds are weaving
A music of sighs:
Arise, arise,
My dove, my beautiful one!

I wait by the cedar tree,
My sister, my love.
White breast of the dove,
My breast shall be your bed.

The pale dew lies
Like a veil on my head.
My fair one, my fair dove,
Arise, arise!

XV

From dewy dreams, my soul, arise,
  From love's deep slumber and from death,
For lo! the trees are full of sighs
  Whose leaves the morn admonisheth.

Eastward the gradual dawn prevails
  Where softly burning fires appear,
Making to tremble all those veils
  Of grey and golden gossamer.

While sweetly, gently, secretly,
  The flowery bells of morn are stirred
And the wise choirs of faery
  Begin (innumerous!) to be heard.

XVI

O cool is the valley now
   And there, love, will we go
For many a choir is singing now
   Where Love did sometime go.
And hear you not the thrushes calling,
   Calling us away?
O cool and pleasant is the valley
   And there, love, will we stay.

XVII

Because your voice was at my side
  I gave him pain,
Because within my hand I held
  Your hand again.

There is no word nor any sign
  Can make amend –
He is a stranger to me now
  Who was my friend.

XVIII

O sweetheart, hear you
  Your lover's tale;
A man shall have sorrow
  When friends him fail.

For he shall know then
  Friends be untrue
And a little ashes
  Their words come to.

But one unto him
  Will softly move
And softly woo him
  In ways of love.

His hand is under
  Her smooth round breast;
So he who has sorrow
  Shall have rest.

XIX

Be not sad because all men
   Prefer a lying clamour before you :
Sweetheart, be at peace again –
   Can they dishonour you ?

They are sadder than all tears;
   Their lives ascend as a continual sigh.
Proudly answer to their tears :
   As they deny, deny.

XX

In the dark pinewood
 I would we lay,
In deep cool shadow
 At noon of day.

How sweet to lie there,
 Sweet to kiss,
Where the great pine forest
 Enaisled is!

Thy kiss descending
 Sweeter were
With a soft tumult
 Of thy hair.

O, unto the pinewood
 At noon of day
Come with me now,
 Sweet love, away.

XXI

He who hath glory lost nor hath
   Found any soul to fellow his,
Among his foes in scorn and wrath
   Holding to ancient nobleness,
That high unconsortable one –
His love is his companion.

XXII

Of that so sweet imprisonment
   My soul, dearest, is fain –
Soft arms that woo me to relent
   And woo me to detain.
Ah, could they ever hold me there,
Gladly were I a prisoner!

Dearest, through interwoven arms
   By love made tremulous,
That night allures me where alarms
   Nowise may trouble us
But sleep to dreamier sleep be wed
Where soul with soul lies prisoned.

XXIII

This heart that flutters near my heart
  My hope and all my riches is,
Unhappy when we draw apart
  And happy between kiss and kiss;
My hope and all my riches – yes! –
And all my happiness.

For there, as in some mossy nest
  The wrens will divers treasures keep,
I laid those treasures I possessed
  Ere that mine eyes had learned to weep.
Shall we not be as wise as they
Though love live but a day?

XXIV

Silently she's combing,
  Combing her long hair,
Silently and graciously,
  With many a pretty air.

The sun is in the willow leaves
  And on the dappled grass
And still she's combing her long hair
  Before the lookingglass.

I pray you, cease to comb out,
  Comb out your long hair,
For I have heard of witchery
  Under a pretty air,

That makes as one thing to the lover
  Staying and going hence,
All fair, with many a pretty air
  And many a negligence.

'XV

ightly come or lightly go
  Though thy heart presage thee woe,
'ales and many a wasted sun,
  Oread let thy laughter run
ill the irreverent mountain air
ipple all thy flying hair.

ightly, lightly – ever so :
  Clouds that wrap the vales below
.t the hour of evenstar
  Lowliest attendants are :
ove and laughter songconfessed
Vhen the heart is heaviest.

XXVI

Thou leanest to the shell of night,
Dear lady, a divining ear.
In that soft choiring of delight
What sound hath made thy heart to fear?
Seemed it of rivers rushing forth
From the grey deserts of the north?

That mood of thine, O timorous,
Is his, if thou but scan it well,
Who a mad tale bequeaths to us
At ghosting hour conjurable –
And all for some strange name he read
In Purchas or in Holinshed.

XXVII

Though I thy Mithridates were
   Framed to defy the poisondart,
Yet must thou fold me unaware
   To know the rapture of thy heart
And I but render and confess
The malice of thy tenderness.

For elegant and antique phrase,
   Dearest, my lips wax all too wise;
Nor have I known a love whose praise
   Our piping poets solemnise,
Neither a love where may not be
Ever so little falsity.

XXVIII

Gentle lady, do not sing
  Sad songs about the end of love;
Lay aside sadness and sing
  How love that passes is enough.

Sing about the long deep sleep
  Of lovers that are dead and how
In the grave all love shall sleep.
  Love is aweary now.

XXIX

Dear heart, why will you use me so?
  Dear eyes that gently me upbraid
Still are you beautiful – but O,
  How is your beauty raimented!

Through the clear mirror of your eyes,
  Through the soft sigh of kiss to kiss,
Desolate winds assail with cries
  The shadowy garden where love is.

And soon shall love dissolved be
  When over us the wild winds blow –
But you, dear love, too dear to me,
  Alas! why will you use me so?

XXX

Love came to us in time gone by
  When one at twilight shyly played
And one in fear was standing nigh –
  For love at first is all afraid.

We were grave lovers. Love is past
  That had his sweet hours many a one.
Welcome to us now at the last
  The ways that we shall go upon.

XXXI

O, it was out by Donnycarney
  When the bat flew from tree to tree
My love and I did walk together
  And sweet were the words she said to me.

Along with us the summer wind
  Went murmuring – O, happily! –
But softer than the breath of summer
  Was the kiss she gave to me.

XXXII

Rain has fallen all the day
    O come among the laden trees.
The leaves lie thick upon the way
    Of memories.

Staying a little by the way
    Of memories shall we depart.
Come, my beloved, where I may
    Speak to your heart.

XXXIII

Now, O now, in this brown land
   Where Love did so sweet music make
We two shall wander, hand in hand,
   Forbearing for old friendship' sake
Nor grieve because our love was gay
Which now is ended in this way.

A rogue in red and yellow dress
   Is knocking, knocking at the tree
And all around our loneliness
   The wind is whistling merrily.
The leaves – they do not sigh at all
When the year takes them in the fall.

Now, O now, we hear no more
   The vilanelle and roundelay!
Yet will we kiss, sweetheart, before
   We take sad leave at close of day.
Grieve not, sweetheart, for anything –
The year, the year is gathering.

XXXIV

Sleep now, O sleep now,
  O you unquiet heart!
A voice crying 'Sleep now'
  Is heard in my heart.

The voice of the winter
  Is heard at the door.
O sleep for the winter
  Is crying 'Sleep no more!'

My kiss will give peace now
  And quiet to your heart –
Sleep on in peace now,
  O you unquiet heart!

XXXV

All day I hear the noise of waters
  Making moan
Sad as the seabird is when going
  Forth alone
He hears the winds cry to the waters'
  Monotone.

The grey winds, the cold winds are blowing
  Where I go.
I hear the noise of many waters
  Far below.
All day, all night, I hear them flowing
  To and fro.

XXXVI

I hear an army charging upon the land
And the thunder of horses plunging, foam about their knees.
Arrogant, in black armour, behind them stand,
Disdaining the reins, with fluttering whips, the charioteers.

They cry unto the night their battlename:
I moan in sleep when I hear afar their whirling laughter.
They cleave the gloom of dreams, a blinding flame,
Clanging, clanging upon the heart as upon an anvil.

They come shaking in triumph their long green hair:
They come out of the sea and run shouting by the shore.
My heart, have you no wisdom thus to despair?
My love, my love, my love, why have you left me alone?

SELECTED BIBLIOGRAPHY

A list of the principal works of James Joyce with the dates of their first appearance.

CHAMBER MUSIC (Elkin Mathews, London, 1907)

DUBLINERS (Grant Richards, London, 1914)

A PORTRAIT OF THE ARTIST AS A YOUNG MAN (The Egoist Press, London, 1916)

EXILES (Grant Richards, London, 1918)

ULYSSES (Shakespeare & Co., Sylvia Beach, Paris, 1922; John Rodker, Paris, for the Egoist Press, London, 1922; The Bodley Head, London, 1936)

POMES PENYEACH (Shakespeare & Co., Paris, 1927; Faber & Faber, London, 1933)

FINNEGANS WAKE (Faber & Faber, London, 1939)

STEPHEN HERO, edited and with an Introduction by Theodore Spencer (Jonathan Cape, London, 1944)

THE AUTHOR

James Joyce was born in Dublin in 1882 into a large and poor family. After graduating from University College, Dublin, he went to Paris in 1902 where he studied medicine. He returned to Dublin and published a few stories, but could not make a living and emigrated with his wife to Trieste in 1905. *Dubliners,* his collection of short stories, appeared in 1914 after being delayed for nine years while Joyce argued with his publishers about the cuts they demanded. *A Portrait of the Artist* was serialized on Ezra Pound's recommendation in the *Egoist* in 1914 and published in 1916. At this time Joyce was under 'free arrest' in Austria but was allowed to go to Zurich where he formed a company of Irish players who performed his play *Exiles* in 1918. Joyce had begun *Ulysses* in 1914; it was serialized by the New York *Little Review* in 1918 but was banned in 1920 after a prosecution launched by the Society for the Suppression of Vice. Turned down by numerous English publishers, *Ulysses* was finally published in Paris in 1922 on Joyce's fortieth birthday. Such was the book's reputation that, despite the ban, reviews began to appear in leading English and American magazines. While some considered it pornography, most of Joyce's literary contemporaries acknowledged it to be a work of genius, one that radically changed the shape of fiction. Though thousands of copies of the book were smuggled into the country, it was not published in England until 1936, long after editions had appeared in German, Czech and Japanese (two versions). In 1922, although harassed by serious eye trouble, Joyce had begun his 'millwheeling vicocyclometer', *Finnegans Wake;* it appeared in fragments as *Work in Progress* in 1927 and was finally published in its complete form in 1939. Eighteen months later Joyce, who had struggled all his life against poverty, ill health and puritanical prejudice, died in Zurich.